W9-CHO-990

CHUCK KLEIN

JIMMY ROLLINS

CURT SCHILLING

PETE ROSE

STEVE CARLTON

ROBIN ROBERTS

SCOTT ROLEN

JIM KONSTANTY

MIKE SCHMIDT

DICK ALLEN

ROBERT PERSON

LENNY DYKSTRA

THE HISTORY OF THE
PHILADELPHIA PHILLIES

MICHAEL E. GOODMAN

CREATIVE EDUCATION

Published by Creative Education, 123 South Broad Street, Mankato, MN 56001

Creative Education is an imprint of The Creative Company.

Designed by Rita Marshall.

Photographs by AllSport (Tim DeFrisco, Rodolfo Ganzales), Associated Press/Wide World Photos,

Icon Sports Media (John McDonough), National Baseball Library, SportsChrome

(Tony Tomsic, Rob Tringali Jr.)

Library of Congress Cataloging-in-Publication Data

Goodman, Michael E. The history of the Philadelphia Phillies / by Michael Goodman.

p. cm. — (Baseball)   ISBN 1-58341-219-0

Summary: Highlights the key personalities and memorable games in the history of

the team that has played in Philadelphia since 1883.

1. Philadelphia Phillies (Baseball team)—History—

Juvenile literature. [1. Philadelphia Phillies (Baseball team)—History.

2. Baseball—History.] I. Title. II. Baseball (Mankato, Minn.).

GV875.P45 G66 2002   796.357'64'0974811—dc21   2001047871

First Edition 9 8 7 6 5 4 3 2 1

IN 1682,

BRITISH QUAKER WILLIAM PENN ESTABLISHED A NEW

colony along the East Coast of the United States as a "holy experiment"

in religious tolerance. He called the settlement Philadelphia, a name

that is Greek for "Brotherly Love." Ninety-four years later, on July 4,

1776, a group of colonial leaders began another experiment in

Philadelphia, adopting a Declaration of Independence from Great

Britain and setting off a revolution.

It was fitting that 100 years later, in 1876, Philadelphia took

another leadership role as the home of one of the first professional

baseball teams in the National League (NL)—the Athletics.

That team soon folded because of financial problems, but a new

NL franchise known as the Phillies was established to stay in 1883.

ED DELAHANTY

No baseball team name has been around as long as the Phillies, and very few sports teams boast such an interesting history.

The Phillies started unimpressively in **1883**, losing their first game 4–3 before a crowd of 1,200.

{SLOW RISE TO THE TOP} Professional baseball in Philadelphia began on April 22, 1876, when the Athletics hosted the Boston Red Stockings in the first game in NL history. Boston won 6–5 before a crowd of about 3,000 fans. Soon both losses and debts piled up for the Athletics, however, and the team was forced to disband before the season ended.

Seven years later, sporting goods manufacturer Alfred Reach purchased an NL club in Worcester, Massachusetts, called the Brown Stockings and moved it to Philadelphia. He renamed the team the Phillies, since it was being relocated to the city commonly known as "Philly." The Phillies got off to a start like that of the Athletics, losing their first game and quickly sinking to the bottom

JOHN KRUK

Grover Cleveland Alexander led the NL in strikeouts every year from **1914** to **1917**.

GROVER ALEXANDER

of the league standings.

The team became an offensive powerhouse in the 1890s, led by future Hall of Fame outfielders Ed Delahanty, Billy Hamilton, and Sam Thompson. Unfortunately, the club had little pitching to go with its great hitting during those days and never finished higher than third place in the NL standings.

Speedy star Sam Thompson set a club record with an amazing 27 triples during the **1894** season.

A lack of pitching haunted the Phillies for years until the arrival of a tall, gangly right-hander named Grover Cleveland Alexander in 1911. In his rookie year, "Alexander the Great" led the NL in wins (28) and shutouts (7). "I'd say that Alexander was the most amazing pitcher in the National League," said legendary outfielder Casey Stengel, who faced the Phillies' ace many times. "He could do wondrous things with the ball. He was the best I batted against."

It took several years to build a strong cast around Alexander,

SAM THOMPSON

Like the great Billy Hamilton, shortstop Jimmy Rollins was a terrific contact hitter.

JIMMY ROLLINS

but by 1915, the Phillies had finally put together enough strong

pitching and hitting to earn their first NL pennant. Alexander led

the league with 31 wins, including 12 shutouts, while

outfielder Gavvy Cravath was the league leader in

home runs (24) and RBI (115).

Unfortunately, the Phils were no match for the

Boston Red Sox and their star pitcher Babe Ruth in

the 1915 World Series, losing four games to one. Philadelphia fans

didn't know it yet, but it would be 35 years before their heroes

would make it to another World Series and 65 years before they

would finally win one.

{ALL HIT, NO PITCH} Led by Alexander's 33 wins in 1916

and 30 in 1917, the Phillies finished second in the NL both years.

Then, before the 1918 season, financial problems forced the Phillies'

owner to sell his star hurler to the Chicago Cubs. It was a turning

Phillies stars Chuck Klein and Dick Bartell played in baseball's very first All-Star Game in **1933**.

12

CHUCK KLEIN

point for the worse for the franchise.

For the next two decades, the Phillies became an amazing "all hit, no pitch" team—especially in 1930. That year, all eight Phillies

regulars batted .280 or better. The club's two top sluggers, outfielders Chuck Klein and Lefty O'Doul, each hit in the .380s.

Klein also smacked 40 homers and 59 doubles while driving in 170 runs. The Phillies' powerful offense was sabotaged by horrible

pitching, however, and the team came in dead last.

The Phils had a disastrous **1942** season, posting a 42–109 record (the worst in club history).

Little by little, Phillies fans started to desert the

team, and the club's owners began to lose money. Top

players were sold or traded away for lesser players

who could be paid lower salaries. Things got so bad

that the league had to take over the debt-ridden team

14

in 1943 and find new owners. Luckily, a wealthy family headed by

businessman Bob Carpenter Jr. from nearby Wilmington, Delaware,

came forward to purchase the club.

The new owners wasted little time in rebuilding the Phillies.

They hired a new general manager, Herb Pennock, and provided

him with money to develop the club's minor-league system. Within

five years, such talented youngsters as outfielders Richie Ashburn

and Del Ennis, shortstop Granny Hamner, and pitcher Robin

DARREN DAULTON

Roberts were brought up to Philadelphia. The young, hungry Phils began a dramatic rise in the standings, going from eighth place in 1947 to third place in 1949. Fans began calling their youthful heroes

the "Whiz Kids" and dreamed of a first-place finish in 1950.

{THE WHIZ KIDS ARE WONDERFUL} Leading the way on the 1950 team was a pair of very different pitchers: 33-year-old reliever Jim Konstanty, who was famous for his tantalizing change-ups, and 24-year-old fireballer Robin Roberts. Konstanty was one of baseball's first closers. In 1950, he made 74 end-of-game appearances, won 16 games, and rang up 22 saves—accomplishments that earned him NL Most Valuable Player (MVP) honors.

Robin Roberts was the NL's best pitcher from **1952** to **1955**, winning at least 23 games per season.

Still, it was Roberts who was the Phils' most important pitching weapon in 1950 and for many more years. Roberts went 20–11 in 1950, the first of six straight years in which he won 20 or more games. Roberts was a very special pitcher. Some opponents considered him downright nasty, and he was never afraid to bust the ball in close to the batter. Mostly, however, Roberts just hated to lose. "I never slept after I lost," he said. "I'd see those base hits over and over in my mind, and they would drive me crazy."

During his Hall of Fame career, Roberts won 286 games. But

ROBIN ROBERTS

Players such as Mike Lieberthal have given the Phillies a reputation for toughness.

Hall-of-Famer Mike Schmidt homered in four straight at-bats in both **1976** and **1979**.

MIKE SCHMIDT

Phillies Player Ever" in 1983. There was no secret to Schmidt's

greatness—it was hard work. "If you could measure time and effort

put in to succeed on the baseball field by dirt on your

uniform," he once said, "mine would be black."

The Phillies of the late 1970s and early '80s had

other stars, too. They included starting pitchers

Jim Lonborg and Jim Kaat, reliever Tug McGraw,

outfielder Greg "the Bull" Luzinski, catcher Bob Boone, and

shortstop Larry Bowa. These players led the club to three

NL Eastern Division titles in a row—1976, 1977, and 1978.

Unfortunately, the Phillies were eliminated in the NL Championship

Series (NLCS) each year.

Then, in 1979, the legendary Pete Rose arrived in Philadelphia

as a free agent to take over at first base. With Rose on board, the

Phillies made another run at a world championship in 1980. This

Bob Boone earned Gold Glove awards as the NL's best defensive backstop in **1978** and **1979**.

25

BOB BOONE

time, they would not be denied.

Rose, baseball's all-time leader in hits, made perhaps his most important contribution in 1980 not at the plate but in the field. It

occurred during the sixth game of the World Series against the

Kansas City Royals. The Phillies were up three games to two and

leading 4–1 in the ninth inning. Then, the Royals loaded the bases off McGraw with only one out. With the tying runs on base, Royals second baseman Frank White hit a pop foul near the stands. Boone camped under it, but the ball bounced out of his glove. Miraculously, Rose was right there to catch the ball before it hit the ground. McGraw struck out the next batter, and the Phillies were finally world champs after 97 years of frustration.

After reaching first base in one **1980** game, Pete Rose stole second base, third base, and home.

{TWO MORE TITLE TRIES} Schmidt, Carlton, and Rose would be around for one more pennant-winning season in 1983, but this time the Phillies were no match for the high-flying Baltimore Orioles in the World Series. Then, during the rest of the 1980s, Philadelphia slowly sank in the NL East standings, finishing in last place in 1988 and 1989.

Several key trades led to a revival in the early 1990s. In came outfielder Lenny Dykstra, first baseman John Kruk, and pitcher

PETE ROSE

Curt Schilling. Phillies management also promoted catcher

Darren Daulton from the minors to take over behind the plate.

Known for his great eye at the plate, Lenny Dykstra drew a team-record 129 walks in **1993**.

Dykstra, who had earned the nickname "Nails" for his hard-as-nails determination with the New York Mets, brought the same intensity to Philadelphia. "He has this winning glow about him that you can see even when he walks through the clubhouse," said Phils pitcher Roger McDowell. "I'm glad I don't have to play against him."

Led by Dykstra, the 1993 Phillies won a club-record 97 games and roared into the World Series against the Toronto Blue Jays. Sadly, after six heart-stopping games—including one wild contest that ended in a 15–14 Toronto win—the Phillies came up short again.

{ROLEN AND ROLLINS RAISE HOPES} New manager Terry Francona laid the groundwork for a Phillies revival in the late 1990s. He began building around such talented young players as

LENNY DYKSTRA

catcher Mike Lieberthal and third baseman Scott Rolen, the

NL Rookie of the Year in 1997 when he hit 21 homers and drove in

92 runs. Then the Phils added speed with outfielders

Doug Glanville and Bobby Abreu and pitching

strength with right-hander Robert Person.

A midseason trade in 2000 sent the talented

but high-priced Curt Schilling to the Arizona

Diamondbacks and brought first baseman Travis Lee to

Philadelphia. Although Lee would help the Phillies rise again,

Francona would not be around to see the improvement. He was

replaced as manager before the 2001 season by former Phillies star

Larry Bowa.

Bowa quickly established a love-hate relationship with his

players. The intense manager often seemed quick to criticize and

slow to praise his players, but he found a way to bring out the best

Scott Rolen had a brilliant all-around year in **1998**, collecting 110 RBI and a Gold Glove award.

29

SCOTT ROLEN

Hard-hitting first baseman Travis Lee was among the Phillies' up-and-coming players.

TRAVIS LEE

Philadelphia's Doug Glanville was one of the fastest center fielders in the National League.

DOUG GLANVILLE

in them. Led by Rolen, Abreu, Glanville, and rookie shortstop

Jimmy Rollins, the Phils made a run at the NL East title for most of

the 2001 season before fading near the end.

Fans hoped for big contributions from second baseman Marlon Anderson in **2003** and beyond.

With a solid nucleus of young players in place,

today's Phillies are hoping to return this historic

franchise to its rightful place among the NL's elite.

Philadelphia fans, often frustrated in the 20th century,

are confident that revolutionary things are just around the corner

for their baseball heroes.

MARLON ANDERSON